Total Chi Fitness

Total Chi Fitness Stretching Exercise for Energy Boost, Ultimate Fitness and Health

By

Sifu William Lee

Author of Amazon Bestsellers

Healing Chi Meditation

5-Minute Chi Boost

T.A.E. Total Attack Elimination

Mind & Body Weapons

And

5-Minute Stress Management

Acknowledgments

To my students and friends. You are all selflessly helping me.

Special thanks to those who asked, insisted and assisted me in turning the seminars in to this practical form.

www.chi-powers.blogspot.cz

Table of Contents

Introduction...1

Real Health From Inside Out 3

Proof is in the Pudding.......................................7

"5-Minute Boost"-Difference............................11

Short History..16

Basic Characteristics 21

Closer Look..26

Quick Look 'Inside' 31

How to Prepare..37

Perfect Mindset...38

Space..39

Chi Breathing 40

Repetition...42

Best Time for Practicing....................................43

How Often 44

Few Rules 45

'Sweet Spot' 46

Total Chi Fitness Exercises 48

Exercise 1 49

Exercise 2 50

Exercise 3 51

Exercise 4 53

Exercise 5 55

Exercise 6 57

Exercise 6A 59

Exercise 7 60

Exercise 8 62

Exercise 9 64

Exercise 10...66

Exercise 11...67

Exercise 12...69

Exercise 13...71

Exercise 14...72

Exercise 15...73

Exercise 16...76

Exercise 17...77

Exercise 18...81

Conclusion...85

Prediction...86

My Promise...87

Introduction

Why Total Chi Fitness?

Today, people are easily overwhelmed by the amount of information's about fitness, exercise, and healthy lifestyle that is thrown at us. Many experts (genuine and otherwise) offer their opinion and methods. Many of those with 'heavy backing' by the mass media are packaged in nearly irresistible ways. The models' sexy bodies and shiny advertisements seem to scream at us:

"Buy this product and become fit and healthy in weeks!"

"Spend your money on this 'gotta-have-it item' and your body will morph into a perfect fitness machine!"

It's easy to get swept away in those streams of 'get fit, strong and sexy quick' messages, because they're practically endless.

For that reason, I think it's fair to honestly warn you:

- This book has nothing to do with those sorts of (mostly false) claims
- You won't need to spend an extra dime on anything – this method demands only a little time and focus
- If you can put aside 18 minutes for 4 to 6 times a week, you will become TRULY fit and healthy
- Sorry, no guarantees of a sexy look :)

Real Health From Inside Out

It's shocking to me (and probably most of you) to see how many people are totally misguided by false claims about getting fit and healthy. You probably know already that powerful industrial lobbies own most of the sports nutrition market, selling millions of types of vitamins, proteins, powders, and pills under different labels. Many of the same people also own or have a hand in mass media messages, magazines and websites that feed the eyes and the minds of the public:

- Fitness is in the muscles
- If you're not ripped or don't even have a six pack, you aren't fit
- Big muscles = strength and health
- You **need** this magic pill, powder, or product to become fit – and sexy!

I could go on for hours like this, but that would be a waste of time. We can't change the world, but we can change ourselves. Allow me to conclude just one more thing. All of the misguided messages and avalanche of fitness marketing could get summed up in one sentence:

"Fitness and health comes from and depends on outside factors."

Wrong, Wrong, WRONG! ... and dangerous for everyone who believes in those claims.

You see, I don't mind as much if fitness industry magnates get richer and richer, if that's what they want to do. But it saddens me to see an endless wave of illusion sold successfully to people. Believe me when I say...

...Most of today's approaches to exercise and fitness are not really healthy!

Why?

In short, because they are aimed at the cardiovascular system and muscles of the body!

What is wrong with that?

Well, a few things for starters. Our good health doesn't JUST depend on the heart, the muscles and the lungs. The healthy functioning of all organs in the body (kidneys, gall bladder, bladder, spleen, long & short intestine, etc.) directly provides us with good fitness level and health. NO health there = NO health at all! That means low energy, and a constant struggle with health. That is no way to achieve any decent fitness level, especially not in the long run.

Another way of showing this principle is through the ancient practice of Chi Kung. Exercises shown and explained in this work are aimed at reviving and maintaining a strong energy flow throughout our gross and subtle bodies*.

Once healthy functioning of the internal organs has been achieved (supported by a lot of Chi and blood flow), we can start enjoying the benefits of total health and fitness in all eleven of our systems: cardiovascular, digestive, endocrine, lymphatic, immune, muscular, nervous, reproductive, respiratory, skeletal, and urinary.

Without having a healthy body on the inside, what is the point of talking about fitness, wellness or enjoying life? I hope you are tracking with me on this. If you are and these words mean something to you, I know you will enjoy this book.

Proof is in the Pudding

Real value is not about what someone says or writes. It is all about (and always was) the practical benefits and results we actually get. In my experience, the reality of life today demands an approach with as much practicality and efficiency as possible. Next to the previously explained differences, efficiency is the most prominent quality of Chi-Fitness exercises that I teach in this book. In the same way as when I teach a seminar or a private class, in this book I focus on practicality and efficiency inside of a process. My goal here, just as in my last book, is not to educate you in theory but in practical terms. You will be provided with a tool that you can use efficiently any time you want. If you do use it, you will be able to generate the same results as thousands of other practitioners – almost without being able to help it. The system is simple yet powerful, and people who use it start feeling the change in a fairly short period. I <u>can</u> promise you that!

Warning: if you started reading this book expecting to see long and 'deep' writing about Chi, meridians, philosophy, or metaphysics (or if you expect to be theoretically entertained), there's bad news. This is the wrong place for those expectations.

However, if you are interested to learn a set of powerful and practical exercises, proven to provide the benefits listed below, there is good news. This is definitely a book where practically anyone (regardless of age, type of body, mind set, race, sex etc.) can quickly learn and apply all exercises without the need for anything extra. If that's where your will is aimed, then you are definitely reading appropriate material. Without any 'filler', I will focus on explaining only the necessary matters that will enable you to understand and derive immediate benefits from this set of exercises.

If you are experiencing any of the following symptoms and needs, this Total Chi Fitness Exercise book will definitely help you (and hopefully answer the question, "do I need this book"):

- Lack of energy
- Headache

- Difficulties in maintaining focus
- Feelings of physical weakness
- Mental weakness
- Need to boost your energy level
- Need to boost Sport performance
- Need to boost working / professional performance
- Desire to boost weight loss results
- Need to improve detoxing results
- Suffering from chronic pain
- Allergies
- Difficulty enjoying life without painkillers and/or medication
- High or low blood pressure issues
- Suffering from a digestion disorder
- Need to accelerate healing from illness or surgery
- Desire to prevent the chronic "I am sick and tired" feeling
- Need to boost your libido and sex drive; or
- (Additional benefits described in the next chapter)

Now, everyone who had read my 5-Minute Chi Boost program will recognize this list of benefits. All (except the last one) are listed there as well. So, what is the difference between these two programs?

In order to explain this in detail I need more space and therefore I'll do it right below, in the next chapter.

Total Chi Fitness

"5-Minute Boost"-Difference

Here is the short answer: these are two separate programs. Both work well and help people. Like a good electric razor, one is a total package meant for consistent home use, and the other is the smaller unit meant for traveling. Both are of superb quality, but one gets more done while the smaller one is easier to carry but must be used more frequently. Women might understand when I say that a pre-packaged hair dye works well to touch up color points, but getting a hair dye job done at a real salon will last for weeks longer.

The methods described in my first book, 5-Minute Chi Boost, are very effective, but you don't have to read them to benefit from this book. (You can draw your own conclusions while reading people's comments on the Amazon sales page.) Some of them may be confused about why I am publishing a 'new' book because most people who daily practice its simple routine enjoy the quick rush of a powerful boost of energy.

Naturally, the 5-Minute Chi Boost exercises are not the only healing exercises I teach. The reason for that is actually simple to understand. 5-Minute Chi Boost is a program that does exactly what it promises: boosts your Chi in matter of a few hours or days. From there, the energy level of a busy practitioner only continues to increase. My first book needed to offer the shortest and most beneficial program, so that people could see fast results. However, some people have the need to go deeper, and have more profound and long-term effects on their well-being and health. That is normal.

It is really interesting to read people's emails, because the messages I get from readers are very similar to those I've received over the last 24 years of teaching. I'm actually very happy to hear all those reactions from people that read my first book on Amazon Kindle. Many readers give the identical feedback of the attendees at my 5-Minute Chi Boost seminar, after practicing the simple system for a while.

<u>For example:</u>

"... I like the 5-Minute Chi Boost program. I get (such and such) benefit) when I do it. However, when I forget to do my 'cycle', my problems seems to reappear. Is there anything that has a longer lasting effect?

- *"I feel much better but I want more. My health problems seem to be deep-rooted can you show us something 'stronger'..."*

- *"In your book and in your email you are talking about assistance that is stronger and can help us even more. Where I can read more about that?"*

People ask this question in various ways, conditioned by a range of circumstances in life. A few years back, I received an 18-page letter that essentially elaborated on only one of these questions. My answer always has been and still is the same.

My answer is "Yes", but you have to use common sense. No one can expect an instant 'magical' solution for a problem or a set of problems that have bothered you for several years or even decades. In the same way as I teach my students, I invite you to further expand the power and potency of the traditional art of Chi Kung. This book outlines complete Chi Kung exercises that have helped people for thousands of years – no question about that. They will also help you if you do them correctly. The learning curve is short, normally one or two weeks. However, you will need to set aside more time for doing them – not just five minutes. Not to worry, it doesn't take a lot more time! Once learned, you can complete one Total Chi Fitness exercise set in about 15 to 20 minutes, and there is no need to repeat the cycle more than once.

As you can see in later chapters, the Total Chi Fitness program is fairly simple to perform and easy to learn. This routine influences each and every energy channel of the body, and can generate results that the 5-Minute Chi Boost program can't offer to most practitioners. The main differences or additional benefits of Total Chi Fitness exercises are:

- Direct and stronger impact on root cause of health problems
- Higher strength for disease prevention
- Longer lasting effects on subtle and physical body

Simply speaking, these Total Chi Fitness Exercises are more profound and have longer lasting effects. The simple 5-Minute Chi Boost method relies on stimulating pressure points and particularly generating a strong flow of life energy. Total Chi Fitness does the same, but by treating all meridians and pressure points on the body. One isn't better than the other – they are simply two programs with the same goals but a different approach. Both can help you and both can heal you. If you have more health problems or if you are serious about preventing weakness, disease, lack of focus, tiredness, headaches (or the other symptoms listed above), I definitely recommend that you learn and start applying this program. If you only need a quick energy boost, just stick to methods described in the previous book.

Short History

This may look like mere theory, but it isn't – I promise. In this short chapter, I offer a few words about the origin of these methods. I also want to share an interesting similarity that I noticed, and that I consider to be a big part of the reason behind the power of this system. Many times, I have read long and boring explanations on this topic just to find out useful information or the scientific proof behind these methods. So, why do these exercises have such a strong positive effect?

We all know that people today suffer from various health problems (disorders, chronic pain, headaches) because of unhealthy lifestyles. Most working men and women today suffer from a low energy level, and often lose the ability to focus. About 1,500 years ago, the 'founder' of these exercises encountered the exact same problem when he compiled this method into an effective and efficient way. Without going into too much detail, this short story sheds some light on how he did it.

Around 500 A.D., a Buddhist monk traveled from India to arrive at the Canton province in China. This monk was not an ordinary monk by any means. He was the third son of Tamil Kalawa, King of Kanchipurnam, one of the biggest and richest regions of India at the time. Before taking vows to renounce his former life in his late thirties, this prince of Kanchipurnam was highly trained by the best teachers. Since he had been chosen to take over the throne, he was able to master the skills given in the secret parts of Atharva and Ayur Veda. After becoming more interested in spiritual advancement, Bodhidharma rejected a political career in India and went to China in order to preach.

Traveling through the Canton province brought him to an original Shaolin monastery (not the modern Shaolin), high in the mountain regions, and hidden from most of the public. He hoped to find there the best prospects for his intended preaching of Buddhism. However, the reality that he met there didn't exactly match with his hopes. The monks he had found were pure and dedicated, but they had neglected the 'illusory' aspects of life, so their bodies were in bad shape. They often fell asleep while meditating due to fatigue, and for this reason, could not achieve their daily goals and duties. (*Sound familiar?*)

While observing these troubling scenes of suffering due to unnecessary health problems (headaches, chronic pains), arrows of sorrow pierced heart of Bodhidarma.

He concluded:

"There is no chance for me to teach spiritual knowledge to people in this condition. First they must heal, and learn how to remain healthy. Then they can be taught martial arts and become strong. After that I can teach them about absolute truth..."

And that was exactly how the next 37 years passed in Shaolin Temple. Bodhidarma was not only able to help them improve their health, energy level, immunity, and all other aspects of physical well-being. He actually transformed that place so that Shaolin became a famous center of Buddhism, well-known throughout all of China.

There are few additional (historically proven) facts you might like to know about. The teachings of the Bodhidarma, monks of Shaolin monastery could preserve and further develop without losing a single drop of effectiveness. Out of dedication to Bodhidarma and the teachings of Buddha, generations of monks in the Shaolin Temple were also able to develop several advanced martial arts systems.

To make a long story short, without Bodhidarma, humanity wouldn't be enriched with disciplines and practices such as acupuncture, acupressure, Tai Chi, Chi Kung, Chinese Traditional Medicine (its larger aspects) or the whole culture of traditional martial arts. From Bodhidarma's training, after healing the inhabitants of Shaolin, the monks were able to develop various martial arts styles such as Wu-Shu, Pa-Kua, Choi Lee Foot, and the traditional five Chinese Kung Fu styles. That's enough history for now. What I will teach you here does not depend on any sort of theoretical knowledge, but I think it's good to learn about the origins of a practice for it to be truly effective.

It is surprising to me (and maybe to you) how similar conditions of completely different lifestyles, separated by 1,500 years, can generate very similar or identical health problems. Some of you may share the excitement of the idea that the same exercises have the same power to destroy sickness and heal the human body today as they have been doing for centuries. It amazes me today the same as it did 42 years ago, when I decided to study the ancient art of Chi Kung and the traditional martial arts of China.

Sifu William Lee

Basic Characteristics

To keep my promise about direct benefits and practicality, let's take a closer look at the exercises given in this book. As you can see in later chapters, all of the exercises are very nicely described and presented with the help of drawings, so we don't need to cover that ground in this chapter. Here, I would like to point your attention towards the specific characteristics of this system in order to help you understand it better.

I'm fairly sure that most of you have already been introduced to the basic concepts of life energy. Different cultures and traditions have different names for the same energy behind everything that we see around us. That force is all pervading, the essential and basic principle of this material creation. In Chinese culture, that energy or principal is called Chi. Although I understand that names are not important as practical actions, we have to use some sort of terminology.

1. UNIVERSAL – MEANT FOR EVERYONE

Before making any further explanations, the first thing we have to clear up is this. If we agree on this, we will accelerate your ability to fully and quickly get the maximum benefit out of this system. Terms such as 'living force', energy of life, biofield, Ki, Prana or Chi (the term I obviously use in this book), are simply different names for the same, the one and only cosmic energy that is present all around us - inside and outside of our bodies. Having said that, the first characteristic of the Total Chi Fitness exercise program can be simply characterized as universal, or meant for everyone.

Therefore:

- Regardless of the place where you live
- Regardless of your age
- Regardless of your financial situation (it has no impact on your ability to get the best out of this program)
- Regardless of your occupation, nationality, religion or beliefs

- Regardless of your previous experience with similar programs, tai chi , chi kung or holistic medicine...

.... Total Chi Fitness exercises are meant for you to use them. Please read quickly again through the lists here* and here*. If you see there any kinds of health issues or needs that resembles your need, be sure that these exercises have the power to help you.

1. – 99 % - EFFECTIVE

No, these exercises are not one hundred percent effective, but 99% is realistic even if you think otherwise. Let me explain it in simple words. If you learn to do these exercises consistently in the proper way, you are on the safe side, the 99% side.

There is only one possibility of failure with Total Chi Fitness exercises. Actually, there are two possibilities:

First is to do them in an incorrect way and therefore not achieve the full and complete effect.

Second is simply not doing them or not practicing regularly.

Unfortunately, there are people who (for some reason or another) are not able to keep up promises they have made to themselves. I'm always sad to see people fail to get the benefits of these teachings. When I speak to them or we trade emails, what always comes up is that they actually could not find enough willpower to set aside 15 to 20 minutes for their own health and well-being. As you can imagine, the percentage is very low, but it is still very discouraging to see some people unable to 'move toward the light' even when it is so easy.

2. EASY / QUICK TO LEARN AND APPLY

The exercises that you know (most of them) are performed in movement. That is not the case with the exercises presented in the Total Chi Fitness system. These exercises all rely on static positions of the body. Although static from the outside, huge changes take place in our bodies when we do them. (More on this later.) What I'm trying to explain here is that because these are stationary positions of the body, the whole system is easy to learn and apply. This point was covered earlier, but because it is so important, let me repeat:

Learning curve: This really depends on how attentive you are and how much time you can dedicate to learning these exercises. On average, however, it does not take longer than one or two weeks at maximum, to run through a complete set of Total Chi Fitness exercises.

How Much Time: Though it's subjective, once you learn and get used to the Total Chi Fitness program, you will need only 12 to 18 minutes to complete the full set. Again, there is no need to repeat sets one after another, as in other systems. In cases of severe conditions or health disorders, some people do practice the Total Chi Fitness exercises even 2-3 times per day (not needed/recommended for most).

Closer Look

In order to explain why these exercises actually work so well, we must have some basic idea about Chinese traditional medicine. Chinese holistic medicine (along with others) teaches that along with the gross aspect of the material body, another and more crucial aspect exists for the proper functioning of our bodies. This 'subtle' aspect is characterized by energy circulating throughout our body. Regardless of the name we use for it, this life energy travels inside our bodies through channels named 'meridians'. The main channels of energy flow connect our main organs and bowels, and secondary channels branch out of the main ones, covering all other areas of the body. This network of energy channels forms a coherent system that facilitates a free flow of energy throughout the body in cycles.

Each meridian is associated with one of the main organs (or the bowels). Proper and complete functioning of a particular organ directly depends on healthy energy flow through that channel. There are twelve main meridians that are symmetrically positioned on both sides of the body. Chi (the life force) travels through the body in cycles of approximately 2 hours. Each organ has a particular time of the day (a 2-hour long cycle) when all other energy channels support its functioning. For example: the stomach has its particular cycle in the morning when it is necessary to digest the most important meal of the day - breakfast. During the night, the liver has its cycle when it is important to rest the body and cleanse it from toxins. Some common misunderstandings can come up even from the teachings of people accepted as authorities in disciplines such as acupressure, acupuncture, Tai Chi, Chi Kung, or related subject matters. I really do not want to speak against anyone here, but in my opinion it's quite essential to clear up this widely spread misunderstanding.

As you can see in this graph below, all main meridians of the body are presented there. The meridians are traditionally presented as traveling on the surface of the body – that was and still is the only way to present them. The misunderstanding, which I will try to explain, is born out of ignorance about the actual positioning of the meridians that begin from inside the body, out of particular organs, that then travel across the body towards the surface. Graphical presentations of energy channels do not cover these aspects of the puzzle, so people who do not really have contact with an authentic line of knowledge have often failed to understand this simple yet very important point. Having explained that, we can easily imagine how energy channels travel from inside the body toward the outside.

Human body meridians

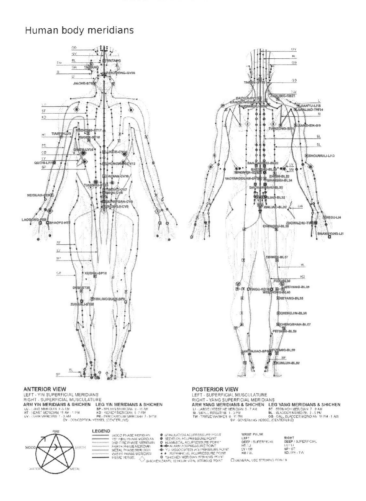

Disciplines like acupressure, reflexology, and acupuncture use this 'energy channels map' in order to influence energy flow within a particular meridian. Well-taught and expert practitioners have great success in treating practically any sort of disease or disorder, simply because it gives the ability to influence and manipulate energy level where and as needed. In a broad sense, we do the same when practicing Total Chi Fitness exercises, but we do not need to spend 10 to 15 years studying and practicing Chinese medicine. We do not need needles, herbs, tools or anything other than 15 minutes of time.

Quick Look 'Inside'

So, how do these exercises influence the flow of energy? How can exercises induce strength and intensity within energy flow?

In the previous chapter, I explained the proper understanding about meridian positioning. Now, in order to explain what these exercises are all about and how they work I have to ask you another thing: please imagine a meridian from inside as if it were a highway. The energy channel is just like a busy six-lane or eight-lane highway, with some lanes going one direction and others headed the opposite way. Hundreds of thousands of 'vehicles' travel both ways, up-and-down, and you can see the red lights when the 'vehicles' have started to slow to a crawl. Each and every part of the body needs a particular amount of energy and meridians are the 'highways' used to supply it to them. Can I ask you now, what happens on the highway when one, two, or three lanes get blocked? Nearly everyone has had the experience of being trapped in a line of cars or buses, and it's a nightmare. You'd almost make more progress if you were walking! Crazy, isn't it?

Blocked energy channels work the same way. Through the partially blocked meridian, energy flows slowly or erratically, and in much smaller amounts then necessary. If blocked meridians are not treated in time, or this happens frequently, the result is pain and disease. If a channel becomes entirely blocked, we face serious health problem and possibly death to the material body. By practicing exercises shown in this book, we can learn how to efficiently unblock the meridians. Don't worry, there is no need for you to study particular meridians, pressure points, or anything complicated.

For another illustration, this process is the same as switching on the light. When you press the button and turn on a light at home, you simply depend on that action for a result. You do not need to know how electricity is made, where it is stored and how it is transported to your town (or your house). You can successfully turn the light off and on as many times you want, once you learn how it is done. (Toddlers do this frequently.) Allow me to say that we all need to learn the process of 'turning on the light'. Many situations in life result in a bigger or smaller block on a particular energy channel. This book is not about any particular disease but it is about health. You can believe me or not, but in order to become healthy, full of energy and enthusiasm for life, you do not need to know a single thing about disease. What you need to know is how to prevent and heal disease.

Even if you were to become totally healthy, without a single block in your body (a near miracle in this modern way of life), the Total Chi Fitness program would still help you. The benefits come because the Total Chi Fitness program ensures that proper Chi flow inside a body continues, therefore preventing blocks from appearing in the future.

Solving the 'Hidden Obstacle'

Just as in the previous book, there are a few things to recommend to maximize the facts of this program. There is nothing hard or complicated about addressing the issue called the 'hidden obstacle', which will be explained.

Before that happens, I have to admit that dealing with this 'hidden obstacle' is not addressed in the traditional scriptures - my Sifu's did not teach me about this. This is probably the one and only thing I teach that is not documented by the scriptures or the Great Masters of history. I'll get to why in a moment.

First of all, what is the 'hidden obstacle'? This is no mumbo-jumbo and nothing unknown. This 'hidden obstacle' is nothing more than complacency. I'm not referring to the usual type of the negative state of mind named complacency. This one is 'hidden' behind the positivity flag of 'it's all good and well' kinds of feelings. I will try to explain this a bit more, since this understanding may possibly benefit you in other aspects of life besides health and fitness.

We all know that being complacent (the first or second variety) is not a desirable 'place', regardless of what we desire or plan to do. When you try to regularly perform any sort of positive activity, complacency can be a serious obstacle for achieving full success. This obstacle is able to keep you back from getting any benefit out of this program, despite the fact that it is a very powerful energy rejuvenation program. This is why I call complacency the 'hidden obstacle', veiled from the eyes of men and women. People who do my 5-Minute Chi Boost program and other powerful energy exercises sometimes face the same issue. Let's explain why this can happen, so that you will be able to respond properly and on time.

The whole 'problem' is that the techniques of this program are simply too effective for the average mindset of a Westerner! In other words, people raised in Western cultures and affected by consumerism react strangely when something easy delivers an immediate result or benefit to them. Anyone raised in the Western culture sees that as normal and common sense - and here comes the biggest problem;

"Because it already gave me a benefit (or I already have what I paid for), there's no need for me to do anything about it anymore!"

Since Total Chi Fitness Exercises quickly deliver results that people want, sometimes they stop doing them regularly out of complacency. You see, for people raised in Chinese or traditional Vedic culture, this is not really an issue – steadiness and discipline traits were (and still are) very natural to them. That is why dealing with this obstacle is probably the only thing I teach that is not explained in scriptures. The mindset of the average men and women in the Western hemisphere is quite different. When we start practicing, the results appear in a short time frame and in various forms (relief from pain, feeling of freshness, more energy, better ability to concentrate). Of course that it is what we want, but if people only focus on the immediate results rather than the process, it could lead to the unwanted habit of complacency.

Please understand: If you stop this program too soon, the Chi flow will not be completely revived. Blockages from your meridians and different parts of your body will not be completely removed. For this reason, the Total Chi Fitness Exercise program would not be able to rejuvenate your life energy completely. That is not necessarily the problem, especially in cases of light health disorders, but even then it is much better to continue practicing the program to be sure that you are getting permanent results. In case of deep-rooted health problems or disorders, stopping early is really the *worst thing* one can do. It is now safe to conclude that this obstacle is not 'hidden' anymore. That makes it easier to deal with effectively.

How to Prepare

Now, since we are clear about the obstacles that can meet us, let's prepare ourselves for efficient execution of the exercises. Put worry aside, there is nothing complicated here nor will you be required to do anything special in order to learn and execute the Total Chi Fitness program. Nevertheless there are few things that will help:

Perfect Mindset

In the same ways as any other activity meant to help you from within, you must start practicing with a mind in as peaceful a state as possible. However, there is no need for meditation or relaxation before practicing Total Chi Fitness. Simply try to generate in your mind the clear intention of having a sharp and clear focus in the next 15 minutes or so. That is all the preparation you need, because once Chi starts to flow, it will become easier and easier to focus and concentrate. After all, we all tend to pay attention to those things that make us feel good. It's as simple as that.

Space

Again, nothing special needed. You need any type of space where you can peacefully practice, because there is no jumping or running involved - nothing bigger than 4 m^2. In a normal house, the room in a small office is more than enough, as long as it has enough light and fresh air. Most importantly, make sure you won't be disturbed for the next 15 minutes at least.

Chi Breathing

In Total Chi Fitness, we use abdominal breathing technique, the most effective for this type of program. In case you have never read anything about yoga, Chi Kung, or breathing exercises, let me describe it.

Abdominal breathing is a very simple and natural way to breathe - newborn babies are perfect examples. Many books are written about the benefits of deep abdominal breathing yet in fact you only need to know this:

- Touch the upper palate with the tip of your tongue and keep it there.
- Exhale all the air out of your lungs in order to prepare.
- Slowly start breathing in through your nose.
- Push out your abdomen slowly, allowing the lower part of your lungs to be filled with fresh air.
- Once your abdomen is completely out (your diaphragm pushed downwards) do not

continue filling the upper part of lungs with air but...

- Slowly exhale through your mouth while squeezing your abdomen and lifting your diaphragm upwards.

There must be no contractions and you should be relaxed and calm. As much as you apply and pay attention to this breathing technique, is how much it will become natural to you. Very soon you will find yourself breathing in this way anytime you feel the lack of energy, stress, fear, or simply an unnatural position or energy imbalance around yo

Repetition

Start with eight repetitions (or keep the position for 8 seconds). Both sides, each exercise. Once you learn all the exercises well you can decide to intensify.

Your body will tell you exactly if you need more or not. Normally people feel comfortable within 12-15 seconds. Adding the repetitions/seconds will progressively enlarge the total time span of your exercise session and its benefits. That is completely up to you of course, but you should know:

- You shouldn't add repetitions before you learn and feel completely comfortable with the Total Chi Fitness program.
- Average number for learning is 8.
- Average number for regular practice is 12 to 15 repetitions.
- Do not increase reps above 30. If you feel you need more power, do 2 sets per day.

Best Time for Practicing

The best time for nearly everyone is in the morning – it has the best impact and strong energy flow will sustain you throughout the whole day.

You can practice around noon and afternoon as well. Many people do. However, you should know that most of people are unable to fall to sleep right after exercising. Give yourself at least two hours after practicing the Total Chi Fitness program – I doubt you will be able to sleep sooner than that.

How Often

Total Chi Fitness exercises can be practiced every day; there is no problem with that. Most practitioners choose to do them 4 to 5 times per week. In my experience, three times a week is still acceptable, but fewer than will significantly postpone the best effects.

Few Rules

'Rules' is probably not the perfect word, but there are a few things to keep in mind while practicing these exercises:

1. Move from position to position slowly, no quick or sudden movements are needed.
2. With two-sided exercises, always start with the left side and then the right.
3. Keep breathing deeply and naturally (it is best to use the simple abdominal breathing technique described above).
4. Always: keep your tongue touching the upper palate.

The next point, which I consider most important, we can also call a 'rule'.

I call it ...

'

'Sweet Spot'

'Rule' or not, first understand what this is and then find your 'Sweet Spot'. This is very important but not at all difficult.

It's all about the intensity of stretching. When you stretch there is a pain. Too much pain is bad because the body shuts down its ability to respond to these exercises. The whole point is to relax, stretch, and so facilitate strong energy flow. On the other hand, if you do not feel pain, this means that you do not stretch enough or that you are so flexible that you feel no pain. However, even if you are very flexible on some areas of your body, you will feel more pain than on some other areas of your body - that is natural.

You have to stretch just to a borderline of your pain tolerance, never go too much above. If you do that it will cause an opposite effect. As the muscles relax, you can find your 'sweet spot' where you feel a certain amount of 'comfy' pain while stretching.

From there you can intensify over time. Please first of all read all instructions for each exercise, try to apply everything and you will soon reap the benefits. In case you are not sure about anything you have a link to a video I provide in later chapters.

Total Chi Fitness Exercises

Exercise 1

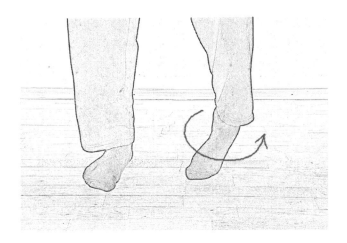

Stand with your spine straight. Keeping your toe on the flow, rotate your ankle outward. Keeping your body weight off the rotating ankle, you will be able to form nice, wide circles. Start with 8 reps, left side first.

Remember:

Keep touching the upper palate with your tongue.

Breathe deeply and naturally.

Exercise 2

This position allows you a maximum stretch of leg biceps and the calf area of your legs. You can use something to lean your weight on (wall, doors or partner). That will allow you to stretch even more.

Remember:

Keep touching the upper palate with your tongue.

Sifu William Lee

Breathe deeply and naturally.

Exercise 3

Form the 'T stance position' with your feet – with the toes of your left foot pointing straight, and your right foot forming a 90° angle. Your shoulders have to parallel the direction of your right foot, and you have to face the same direction as your left foot.

Placing left palm little below left knee and right one little bit above the knee, start moving your chin as near possible towards your knee.

Lift the fingers on your left foot up, keeping the weight on your left heel. Keep your fingers up while moving your chin toward the knee.

Find your 'sweet spot'. Keep that position for 8 seconds. Repeat the same on the right side.

Remember:

Keep touching the upper palate with your tongue.
Breathe deeply and naturally.

Exercise 4

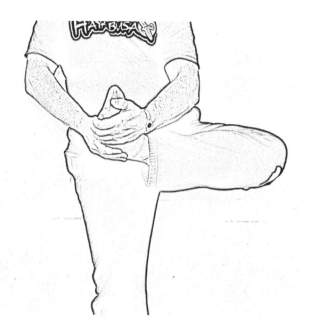

Lift your leg up, while holding your left foot with both hands. Keep your upper body and spine straight. You can then lean your back on something in order to help you keep balance.

Hold the position for 8 seconds. Repeat the same on the right side.

Remember:

Keep touching the upper palate with your tongue.

Breathe deeply and naturally.

Exercise 5

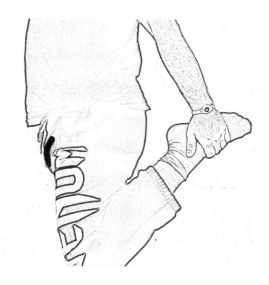

Fold your leg as shown, and stretch. Move your knee as much as possible towards the back. You can use the help of a partner, wall or any solid object near you in order to keep a better balance.

Hold the position for 8 seconds. Repeat the same on the right side.

Remember:

Keep touching the upper palate with your tongue.

Breathe deeply and naturally.

Exercise 6

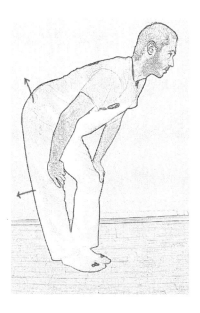

Keep your feet together and your knees straight. Bend forward, and place both palms on your knees. While placing 80% of your body weight on one leg, keep it   as straight as possible while bending slightly to the other side, like when you walk. The hip on the side of the stretched leg will naturally move upwards, stretching all the muscles around the hip and lower back area.

Switch between the legs, keeping the stretching position for 2-3 seconds.

Repeat 8 times, and then switch to the next exercise without changing the position of the body.

Remember:

Keep touching the upper palate with your tongue.

Breathe deeply and naturally.

Exercise 6A

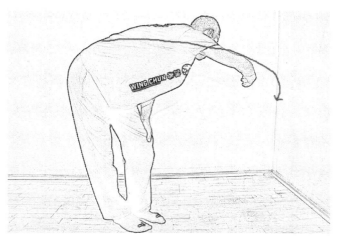

Keep your right knee stretched and extend you right arm as shown, as far as possible to the left side of your body. Experiment to find the angle where you stretch the most.

Switch sides, keeping the extreme stretching position for 2-3 seconds.

Remember:

Keep touching the upper palate with your tongue.

Breathe deeply and naturally.

Exercise 7

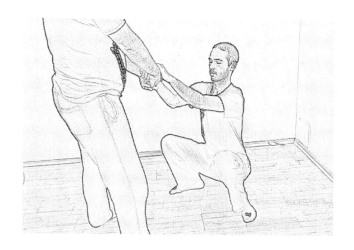

For this exercise and the next, you will need help. If you do not have a partner, find a door, a piece of stiff cardboard, or any other object that can safely hold a portion of your weight.

Stand straight with your feet parallel. Your stance should be as wide as your shoulders. Keep your spine straight and move slowly into the position as shown.

Once there, relax your lower back and hips. Do not hang on the object, but allow your body to stretch the muscles on both sides of your lumbar spine / lower back area.

Stay in that position for 8 seconds. Slowly rise up while keeping your spine straight.

Remember:

Keep touching the upper palate with your tongue.
Breathe deeply and naturally.

Exercise 8

Again, using the help of the partner or object, prepare by forming the 'V position' with your feet. Your legs still need to be straight.

Stretch your upper body entirely, parallel to ground. Look towards your hands. Stay in that position for 8 seconds.

Remember:

Keep touching the upper palate with your tongue.

Breathe deeply and naturally.

Exercise 9

Your stance should be a bit wider than your shoulders. Place your hands on your hips. Move as shown in order to stretch the inner thigh area.

Keep stretching each side for two or three seconds. Gradually increase the intensity and pressure. Repeat stretching 8 times on each side.

Remember:

Keep touching the upper palate with your tongue.

Breathe deeply and naturally.

Exercise 10

This exercise is performed in many exercise programs and you are probably familiar with it. However, there is a key difference here. While stretching on each side, 'seek the angles' with your hips.

This means that you are not supposed to move only straight left and right, but move your hip at an angle and you will find angles that allow your body extra good stretching of all the involved muscles.

Remember:
Keep touching the upper palate with your tongue. Breathe deeply and naturally.

Sifu William Lee

Exercise 11

This is the classical exercise you are probably familiar with. However there are a few details of difference. Rotate your hips while gradually increasing the diameter of circles/stretching intensity. Keep your head on one place, your spine erect. You should do your cycles only with your hips.

Rotate your hips slowly, three times on the left and three times on the right side - that is one cycle. Do eight cycles.

Remember:

Keep touching the upper palate with your tongue.

Breathe deeply and naturally.

Exercise 12

This one is usually a little bit confusing in the beginning, that's why I explain it with two photos instead of one. The video explains it completely, of course, but in case you are not connected to the Internet you can still clearly understand it from the photos.

Behind your back, catch your left wrist with your right hand. Pull the left hand with your right as much as you can, down and to the side. Simultaneously, shift your neck toward the right side. Keep that position for 8 seconds.

Repeat everything on the opposite side.

Remember:

Keep touching the upper palate with your tongue.
Breathe deeply and naturally.

Exercise 13

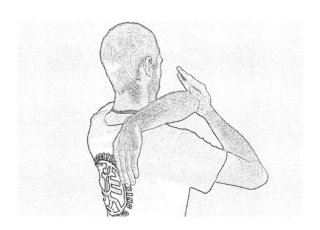

Place your left hand above your right shoulder. Using your right palm, push your left elbow towards the back as much as you can. Stay in that position for 8 seconds.

Remember:

Keep touching the upper palate with your tongue.

Breathe deeply and naturally.

Exercise 14

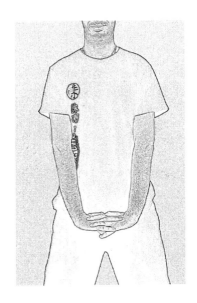

While standing straight, place your palms as shown and then stretch your arms above your head. Keep this position for eight seconds.

Raise your palms above your head, linking the fingers, and keep that position for the next 8 seconds. Simultaneously, relax the neck and shoulders as much as possible.

Exercise 15

Catch your elbow push it behind your head. Keep that position for a second. Repeat the same on opposite side.

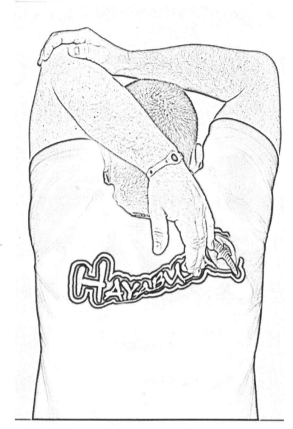

Very slowly lower your arms down.

Remember:

Keep touching the upper palate with your tongue.

Breathe deeply and naturally.

Exercise 16

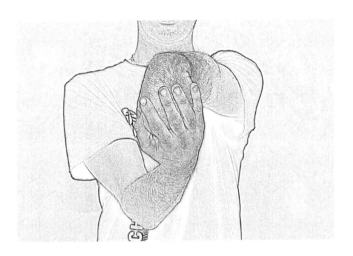

While standing, position your arms in front of you. Using your right hand, push your left palm down and towards the body, as much as you can, while keeping your elbow straight. Hold that position for 8 seconds.

Repeat the same on the opposite side.

Remember:

Keep touching the upper palate with your tongue.

Breathe deeply and naturally.

Exercise 17

This exercise is different from the others. It's not a muscle stretching exercise but it's an exercise that extends the energy flow. By this time, blood and energy will be flowing strongly throughout your body. In this exercise, you must focus your mind on extending the energy out from your arms.

'Energy Burst' 1.

It may be helpful to imagine your arms as the hoses used by firefighters. In your mind's eye, they have to strongly extend, and practically catapult the energy out. Use some spot or object in front of you and simply target it with a strong energy flow bursting out of your fingers.

'Energy Burst' 2.

'Energy Burst' 3.

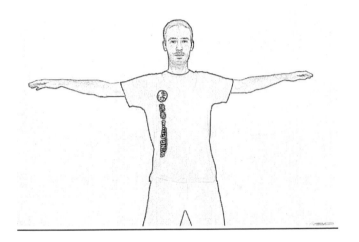

'Energy Burst' 4.

Remember:

Keep touching the upper palate with your tongue.

Breathe deeply and naturally.

Exercise 18

This exercise is the last one and should always be done as the last exercise even when you do not have time to do them all. (Of course, it is always recommended to do all of them, as shown here.) Even if you must finish earlier, try to finish with this exercise. As the centering exercise, it collects life energy within the energy center of your body.

Centering - 'Energy Ball' - Position 1.

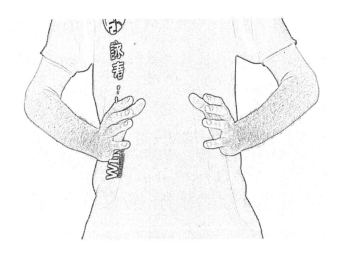

Comfortably take the position as shown. Your palms should be placed no higher than your plexus and no lower than your pubic bone. Moving slowly, your palms should be pushed from and towards each other, as you pay attention to any sensations you can feel between your palms. In the moment that you feel sensation (warm, cold, tension, or anything else), you have found the 'sweet spot' for this exercise.

Focus your attention on that space between your palms and start forming a ball of energy between your palms. You should use your imagination (a ball of shiny white light normally works for everyone) and with each breath you should add more power there, directed into the ball.

Keep this position for eighth breathing cycles. Then moves to the next position.

Centering - 'Energy Ball' - Position 2.

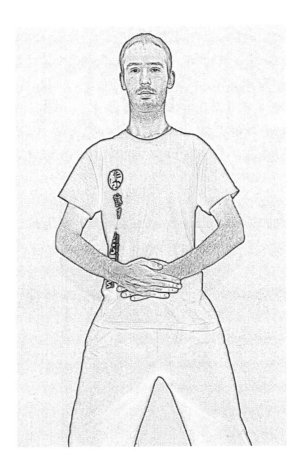

Place your palms on the Tan Tien - this pressure point is exactly on your body's central line, about 3-4 inches below the navel. The left palm covers it directly, as the right palm covers the left one. Bring your attention to the Tan Tien area. Because you're supposed to move your abdomen while breathing most people will have no problem with feeling and focus. If you have difficulties, use the thumb of your left hand and press the Tan Tien area for a few seconds, which will certainly help.

With your attention fully focused, breathe 8 cycles, naturally. Your energy will become centered, properly and completely.

Complete exercise video you can get from http://chi-powers.blogspot.cz/2013/07/video.html here. A bit more about this; there is absolutely 0 complications for you, you don't have need to download anything etc. If you are not online right now while reading this book, you can always visit my blog, find the Total Chi Fitness Video post, subscribe and we will send you a link. There is a necessary procedure, demanded due to anti spam rules etc. - after you confirm your email address, please allow up to 1h for getting the email with the link to the Total Chi Fitness Video. Thank you

Conclusion

Using the photos and the video* I provide, anyone can understand and learn this Total Chi Fitness exercise program in a short time. The learning curve of this program is therefore very short. Before you start, you could be cheated by a false impression that, in someone's head, could sound like this:

"Nothing fancy here, it looks too simple. Can this program be as powerful as this guy claims?"

Do not be cheated by this or any other false concept (or obstacle) that is stopping you from starting this Total Chi Fitness exercise program.

* On http://chi-powers.blogspot.cz/2013/07/video.html you can request out Total Chi Fitness Video.

Prediction

In order to further inspire you, I will like to offer a short but realistic prediction about what awaits you when you start practicing this program:

- It will take a maximum of 5 times for you to start feeling various advantages and positive effects as you do the program.

- In the first 3 weeks of properly doing the Total Chi Fitness exercises, at a minimum of 3 times per week or more, your energy flow will double in strength. You will experience significant relief from tiredness, pain, health disorders, etc.

- After 3 months of following the Total Chi Fitness Program (properly and at a minimum of 3 times per week or more), you will unable to imagine your week WITHOUT it!

The reason I say this is not to infuse any sort of hype. Obviously you purchased this program, and I simply want to make sure that you really use this book and videos so that you can really benefit in health and wellness, sports performance, and all other aspects of life.

My Promise

You may think it's not necessary for me to promise you anything, and if you feel that way, I agree. However, I think some readers may need a slightly stronger 'push' and for that reason I am including my personal promise in the conclusion of this book.

I promise that if you learn these exercises properly and do them at a minimum of 3 times per week:

- You'll never feel like you're losing time and effort.
- You will be surprised at the effectiveness of these exercises.
- You will be more than happy with the various benefits that the Total Chi Fitness program generates for you.
- All promised benefits* will appear gradually, one by one, growing in energy strength, gradually removing all the energy blocks

inside your body and (provided your lifestyle is not opposed to these effects) therefore…

- You will eventually achieve a balanced state of health and wellbeing, and maximize your performance.

How's that for a promise?

And if you *really* <u>can't find</u> 15 minutes a day, if you feel you need something shorter or more 'practical' then please check out my 5-Min Chi Boost book.

It is powerful pressure point treatment program that need's 3x less time (one round takes about 5-6 minutes to complete).

Rest be on you, my friends. To all of you and your dear ones health, I wish best of wealth and wellbeing.

Sincerely,

William Lee

Printed in Great Britain
by Amazon.co.uk, Ltd.,
Marston Gate.